The Gift of Being Peculiar

Written by Micaiah D. Yhisrael

Illustrated by Dariea Shorter

aka Selah

DEDICATION

To Jamiyah,
My most unexpected treasure and peculiar gift.
You were born to stand out and be different.
Never let anyone dim your light.
Shine on!

Mommy loves you more than the stars and the moon and the sun in the sky

Peculiar: adjective. Different to what is normal or expected; strange.
Particular; special.

Exodus 19:5 ...then ye shall be a peculiar treasure unto me above all people:
for all the earth is mine.

Hi, I'm Kenza and I'm a peculiar gift.
My mom calls me a special treasure,
beyond measure,
even my name means treasure in Arabic

Some people think being peculiar is bad or weird.
But my mom is very smart,
and she said being peculiar just means you're
different and special.

I love that!
Being different is awesome,
because it means there is no one else who is just
like me
or just like you.

Mom always says I dance to the beat of a different drum.

HOORAY!!

No, I'm not really dancing.
It just means I'm good at being a leader and
thinking for myself.
I bet you are too!

It's ok if you don't want to be like everyone else.
Mom says some people don't fit in
because they were born to stand out.

You can have your own style of dress and hair.
You can have your own thing,
whatever that may be.
That makes you, You!
And me, ME!

That's all a part of being special or peculiar.
It's like being a snowflake,
No two are alike.
But each one is beautiful.
My mom said people can be the same way.

Some people make fun of people or things that are different or peculiar.
Until they find out being peculiar is like having a super power.
The power to be who and what you want is a super feeling.

My mom says whatever I dream to be I can be, if
I put my mind to it.
The possibilities are endless.
And the same is true for you too!

I don't know exactly what I'll be when I grow up.
Mom said I still have time to decide.
For now, I've decided to be awesome,
courageous and kind,
that's always a good way to be.

Mom says never let anyone make you feel bad
about being yourself.
She said I am fearfully and wonderfully made.
My mom says all children are and that's another
part of being a gift.

My mom says no one can love you as much as you love yourself.
And you should love everything about yourself even if it's not perfect.

So everyday let's tell ourselves:
I am a peculiar treasure.
Blessed beyond measure.
And no matter what anyone may say,
I am unique and beautiful in every single way!

ACKNOWLEDGMENTS

I would like to thank Frances Ruffin, one of my first baby sitters and another mom figure. It was on your lap, next to your bed, listening to you read me stories that started my love of books and reading. I treasured those times dearly.

To Dariea, it takes a special gift to bring words to life. The Most High truly blessed you with amazing talent.
I'm honored to have had you collaborate with me to bring this vision to life, I hope it's not the last. Our children are the future, thanks for giving Kenza a face and an amazing presence.
Add children's book illustrator to your resume.

To all my friends and family thanks for the unending love, encouragement and support.

And to my SCPA family, we were always considered "different and weird" those artistic kids, being normal has always been overrated.
That school may not have been perfect, but it enabled me to be well-rounded and versatile and to showcase and embrace being peculiar.
We will forever be SCPA family.
~Micaiah